Volume I-IV Overview of the Three-Fold Mimesis of Life

How do you perceive yourself?

How do others perceive you?

I0540525

Lived Experiences are the Puzzle pieces to your Mimesis

Your Mimesis is the construct of your reality

Everyone has to figure it out

Your Mimesis is your Reality
When how you perceive yourself
Align with how others perceive you

DR. RONALD BARNES

ISBN: 978-1-971408-06-4 (Paperback)
ISBN: 9681-971408-07-1 (Hardback)
ISBN: 978-1-971408-08-8 (E-book)

Library of Congress Control Number: 2026900036

Printed in the United States of America

Published by:

info@thequippyquill.com
(302) 295-2278

Table of Contents

The Three-Fold Mimesis of Life

Plato and Aristotle

The Purpose of the Three-Fold Mimesis of Life: Background on the author's reason to write the four volumes

The purpose of this book and associated Volumes I-IV is to give input into creating a more productive and better society, congruent with how to give individuals insight into creating a better You, a better Me, a better life. To be honest, what America needs to do to be a better society is to simply adhere to the dogma established by our forefathers (The Constitution of the United States of America, The Declaration of Independence, The Emancipation Proclamation) and the dogma America considers its moral foundation (The Holy Christian Bible). However, there are over 300 million people in America who are diverse in race, culture, and religion. How do you get this number of people to conform, people who are so diverse, so individually different, who have different ideologies? The answer is that even among differences, there are considerable similarities and significant common interests that should be the focus of a great society. Such as:

1) The majority of Americans want to be safe in their environment, in their homes, in their schools, in their communities and frankly everywhere they go.

2) The majority of Americans want to provide for their family.

3) The majority of Americans want to provide quality education opportunities for their children.

4) The majority of Americans want access to quality health care.

5) The majority of Americans want good jobs and equal economic opportunity.

6) The majority of Americans want adequate housing.

7) The majority of Americans want the right to worship the religion of their choice or the right not to worship.

8) The majority of Americans embrace: the right of women to have control over their bodies

9) The majority of Americans want racism and discrimination ended. At least the 84,000,000 Americans who voted for Joe Biden. However, there were 74,000,000 Americans who voted for Donald Trump.

10) The majority of Americans want the opportunity and freedom to pursue their right to life, liberty and the pursuit of happiness. However, while the majority of Americans want these rights and believe they are basic to America and to Democracy, the reality is that these basic human rights are denied to a significant number of Americans.

There are common to the American majority that have nothing to do with diversity differences. The problem is that America does not apply these rights, common to all Americans, to all of its citizens, and America has a long history of denying rights to human beings. Therefore, the citizens of America need to focus on how they, themselves, can determine how to gain access to their inherent rights, denied to them by the general body of America's political, economic, social, and institutional structure. A Better people, a better society, A better America is hypothetical but within America's capability. The general tone of America is determined by American leadership. People tend to be a microcosm of the overall general tone set by leadership. The following information indicates that point.

Too many young people in society are lost during their childhood and adolescent stages in life. They are lost to dysfunctional behavior in themselves, in their family life, and in their friendships and associations. Unhealthy and dysfunctional life experiences during the developmental and adolescent years often cause the in many areas: crime, economics, education, government, global warming, attitude toward other people, health care, law enforcement, the legal system, and the government / political / politicians'

relationship. As a result, society loses. The "I don't care" sentiment has another angle. I don't care about you; I only care about me and people who look and think like me.[1] It is a contagious sentiment and the counterpart of selfishness, greed, often racism, and sometimes low self-esteem, anxiety, and depression that prevents people from having a positive life direction and America's growing mental health crisis. [2] This sentiment has become a significant phenomenon in our so-called "civilized society". Evidence of the dysfunction in our society is visibly displayed for all Americans to witness in the halls of our United States Congress, the government that is supposed to operate in the best interest of the people, consistently behaves in conflict, disagreement, and dysfunction. The news media present information on a daily basis, reflecting dysfunction and the "*I don't care sentiment.* This is not to mention the bribes and activities politicians engage in for their own selfish interests at the expense of the American people. Evidence of American dysfunction is outed on a daily basis. The news media reports daily that people kill people, often for no good reason. Politicians embroil themselves in scandal. The American people are in constant complaint mode. Kids and young adults are depressed and anxiety-ridden about their future.

Dysfunctional exposure has the potential to result in an unproductive life or a life that ends in tragedy or unhappiness, or disappointment. A motivation for this author in writing this series of

Volumes on the Three-Fold Mimesis of Life is the statistical reality that from 2009-2018, there have been 180 school shootings and 356 victims, mostly school-age kids. The totals are even greater since 2018. From the rural areas, the suburban areas, to the urban cities, 114 people were killed and 242 were injured in shootings at K-12 schools from 2009 through 2018. [3] This is the time in a young person's life when they should be thinking about life, about living, learning, enjoying themselves, having fun, developing skills, and being interested in preparation for their future. **HOWEVER,** no way is it normal for kids to become victims of tragedy. **In addition,** the tragedy suffered by innocent and dysfunctional kids can be avoided. **The real tragedy is that the tragedy could have been avoided. Kids killing Kids is the most ridiculous phenomenon in our American society and the biggest failure of America.** That no significant action is taken to remedy the gun violence problem only means the problem is likely to occur again and again. The only remedy to gun violence is significant gun regulation and control. Ideally, worldwide gun elimination is a more certain remedy for peace, worldwide. Every one of these incidents could have been avoided, should not have happened, but they did. Why? The blame must be placed on the perpetrators and the parents of the perpetrators, the gun companies, the gun lobby, and legislators who protect the gun companies at the expense of children's lives. The gun psychology among Americans has to shoulder much of the blame. Somewhere in the kid's socialization developmental process, things went awry. An average of 25-30 school shootings per year have occurred since 2016, and they are increasing. The only benefit of COVID-19 was that with schools closed, there were no school shootings. White students account for most school shootings (approximately 67%). Shootings at mostly white schools have more casualties. [4]

Majority of U.S. teens worry a shooting could happen at their school

% of teens saying they are___ about the possibility of a shooting happening at their school

	Very worried	Somewhat worried	NET
All teens	25	32	57
Boys	22	29	51
Girls	28	35	64
White	20	31	51
Black	27	34	60
Hispanic	37	36	73

Note: Whites and blacks include only single-race non-Hispanics. Hispanics are of any race. Figures may not add to net total due to rounding.
Source: Survey of U.S. teens ages 13 to 17 conducted March 7-April 10, 2018.

PEW RESEARCH CENTER

A majority of U.S. teens, ages 13-17, fear a shooting could happen at their school, and most parents share their concern. Considering, school is supposed to be the safest place for kids next to the home, this is a problem that should be given immediate attention. The security and safety of our children should be the top priority of society. Fifty-seven percent (57%) of teens are worried and concerned about violence happening in their school. Ironically, considering most of the school shootings and school violence occur in White schools, sixty-four percent (64%) of non-White teens express a higher level of concern. Seventy-three percent (73%) of Hispanics indicate they are somewhat worried about violence in their schools. Among girls, sixty-four percent (64%) and boys (51%) say they are very concerned. [5]

Solutions considered to mitigate this problem are focused on mental illness, assault-style weapon bans, and the use of metal detectors in schools as potentially effective. Some people think teachers and school officials should carry guns in schools. The dilemma is what type of learning environment is created when students enter schools through a metal detector or witness teachers carrying guns. Consciously or subconsciously, students think there is potential for violence in the school. Whether shootings occur in school or out of school, none of the proposed solutions will mitigate the problem. America has to create a better environment for its kids. Just as kids learn and develop dysfunctional cognitive inclinations, kids can learn and develop functional inclinations. The learning environment, the school, is the perfect environment to teach kids functional, interactive behaviors. The problem of school violence directly affects schools. It makes sense for schools to take a full-course initiative to mitigate the problem.

Horowitz (2000) advances that:

"Some boys get lost because they are systematically led into a moral wilderness by their experiences at home and on the streets, where they are left to fend for themselves. These are the boys upon whose behalf I testify in court, trying to help judge and jury see the injustice of their experiences and how they have been robbed of their childhood by abusive and neglectful parents, by malevolent drug dealers, and

> *by the sheer viciousness of their daily life. And I argue that to simply punish them with death ... only compounds the injustice imposed upon them by the world in which they grew up".* [6]

The problem with this approach is that it is reactive. Damage to the community, ruined lives, the life of the perpetrator, the victims, their parents, friends, school teachers, school administrators, other students, all lives suffer; some are ruined. The solution to addressing dysfunction in kids should be proactive, not reactive. Spending resources after the fact is shortsighted when resources spent before the fact will have more potential to mitigate the problem. A proactive approach realistically will not eliminate the problem 100% but any significant improvement will potentially save dysfunction, lives, prevent tragedy, and develop a more functional society.

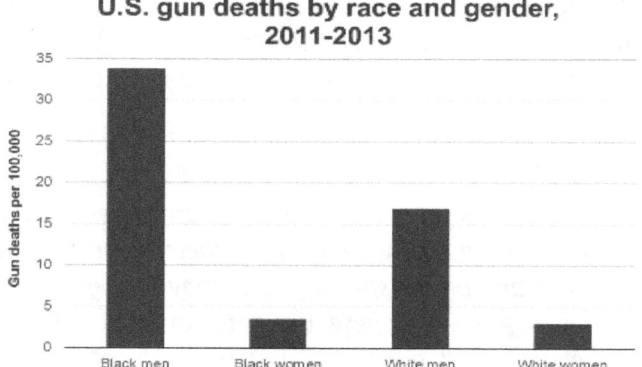

U.S. gun deaths by race and gender, 2011-2013

Note: These figures have all been calculated using a 2011-2013 average to smooth single-year fluctuations.
Source: CDC Injury Prevention & Control database.   BROOKINGS

Focusing on the ultimate cost of dysfunction and bad life choices (premature loss of life), the value of making the right life choices is put into perspective. Black men are at the greatest risk of losing their lives from gun violence. In 2013, firearm deaths accounted for over 11 percent of all years of potential life lost among the black population, but less than 6 percent of all years of potential life lost among the white population.[7] Even more startling is the fact that the useless loss of life among young Black men is much higher than experienced by other races and genders.

In Comparison to other Countries, the U.S. gun death rate was 10.6 per 100,000 people in 2016, the most recent year in the study, which used a somewhat different methodology from the CDC. That was far higher than in countries such as Canada (2.1 per 100,000) and Australia (1.0), as well as European nations such as France (2.7), Germany (0.9), and Spain (0.6). But the rate in the U.S. was much lower than in El Salvador (39.2 per 100,000 people), Venezuela (38.7), Guatemala (32.3), Colombia (25.9), and Honduras (22.5), the study found. Overall, the U.S. ranked 20th in its gun fatality rate that year. [8]

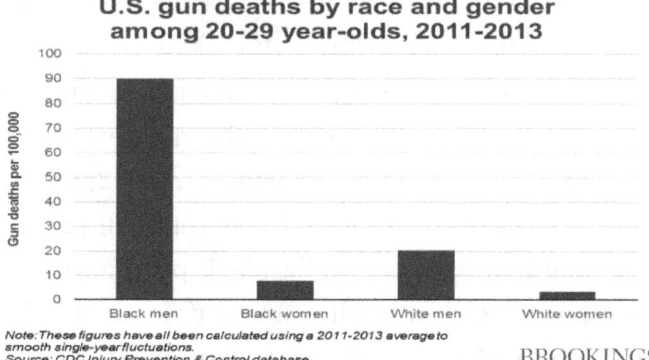

U.S. gun deaths by race and gender among 20-29 year-olds, 2011-2013

Note: These figures have all been calculated using a 2011-2013 average to smooth single-year fluctuations.
Source: CDC Injury Prevention & Control database.

BROOKINGS

However, because Blacks are stereotypically inner-city dwellers and Whites, for the most part, inhabit the suburbs, that does not mean Whites are immune from their share of dysfunction that causes loss of life. Gun deaths vary by type. The vast majority (77 percent) of white gun deaths are suicides, and less than one in five (19 percent) is a homicides. These figures are nearly opposite in the black population, where only 14 percent of gun deaths are suicides but 82 percent are homicides: ironic. [9] If White society is so advantaged, why would their suicide rate be so high compared to the Black population? Surely, if any race has reason to be depressed about their plight in society, it is Black people who live in poverty, in a racist society; mortality rates are higher, and Blacks frequently encounter discrimination, prejudice. It is ironic that Blacks, who have greater reason to be depressed, have a lower suicide rate than Whites.

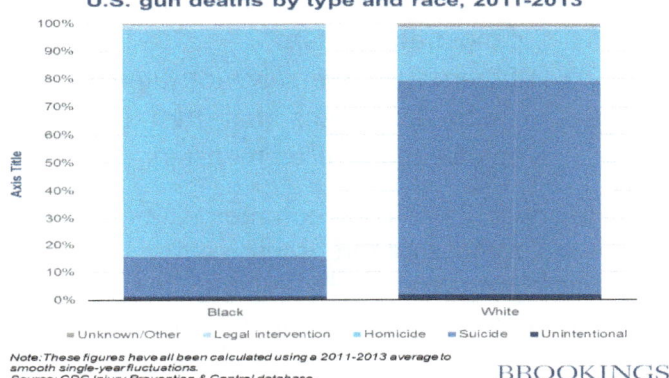

U.S. gun deaths by type and race, 2011-2013

Note: These figures have all been calculated using a 2011-2013 average to smooth single-year fluctuations.
Source: CDC Injury Prevention & Control database.

BROOKINGS

However, the fact remains that incidents and deaths by gun violence are on the rise. A significant number of victims are young people who have not yet begun to live the productive years of their lives.[10] The number of shootings in 2023 has gotten off to a tragic start. [11]

> - Mass shooters are rapidly becoming younger and deadlier in the U.S.
> - Law enforcement agencies and experts say research lags behind the cause of it.
> - New solutions are needed for a rising threat that often lurks in online chats and social media.

It is hypothesized that:

- Some do it out of a perverse desire to make a difference in the world.

- Others are driven by mental illness, pandemic isolation
- Others are perversely motivated by social media influences that turn them into hateful and sadistic monsters.

However, there's one common element among America's mass shooters: their youth. [12] School Shootings perpetrated by young people have become so common and blatant that the police seem to become more fearful, themselves, when they approach a young school shooter. [13]

Gun violence has many negative repercussions in education, health, incarceration, family instability, and social capital. Anxiety levels rise and cognitive functioning worsens among school children following a violent crime within half a mile of their home, and when living in a dysfunctional situation or environment. Blacks are twice as likely as Whites to die from homicide. This fact alone requires Black men and women to focus on making positive decisions in their lived experiences. Individuals who witness violence are at increased risk for a variety of mental health issues, which can manifest as post-traumatic stress disorder, depression, poor academic performance, substance abuse, risky sexual behavior, delinquency, and violent behavior. Phenomena resulting from dysfunction and violence carry a heavy weight in the lived experiences of individuals, especially Black individuals. Gun violence in Black communities is part of a vicious cycle of racial discrimination, inequality in the U.S., reflecting existing social inequalities, and a misdirected, frustrated, aggressive complex. The American reality is that the social psychology and institutional constructs in America make it even more challenging for young black people, especially young black men, to escape poverty and violence.[14] However, the fact remains that regardless of the disadvantages individuals encounter, it should not be and does not have to be a reason for failure in life.

These are not necessarily race problems. Labeling prejudice and discrimination as race problems dilutes the fact that they are society problems. Race should not even factor into the need for identifying solutions to this problem. Minority youth have their share of "kids killing kids (KKK)." Seems that everything KKK is a dysfunctional problem in society. The primary issue is that more focus and attention need to be given to developing positive cognitive stability among our youth. All youth need parental guidance, without which the propensity for dysfunctional behavior increases. The reason it is important to give positive guidance to all children is that even the good kids, raised by good parents, can become victims of dysfunctional kids, deprived of proper guidance. Often, the good kids are victims of school shootings.

School shootings are a real problem in our society. The school should be a safe haven for kids, next to the home. By April 5, 2022, there were 22 school shootings before the end of the fourth month of 2022. It has not even been a full year of schooling.

Schools just opened after the COVID-19 pandemic. There have been 114 school shootings since 2018, when Education Week began tracking such incidents for grades K-12. The highest number of shootings, 34, occurred last year (2021). There were 10 shootings in 2020 and 24 each in 2019 and 2018".[15] Mass shootings in general are on the rise.

> *The most ridiculous thing one could ever imagine in life is the phenomenon of kids killing kids. This is a prime example of failing adult leadership, a failing society, a failing country, and a failing America.*

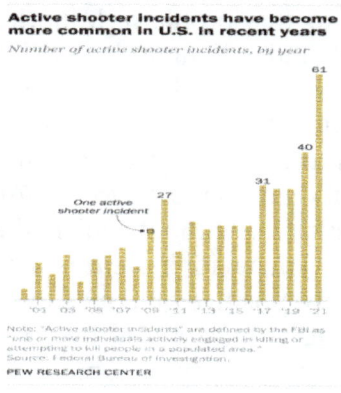

Active shooter incidents have become more common in U.S. in recent years

Number of active shooter incidents, by year

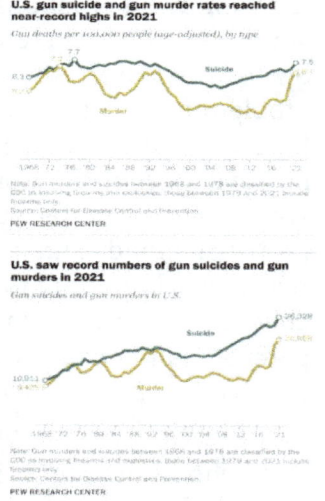

U.S. gun suicide and gun murder rates reached near-record highs in 2021

U.S. saw record numbers of gun suicides and gun murders in 2021

The gun murder rate in the U.S. remains below its peak level (1992) despite rising sharply during the pandemic. There were 6.7 gun murders per 100,000 people (20,958 murders) in 2021, below the 7.2 recorded in 1974. The gun suicide rate, on the other hand, is now on par with its historical peak.level (1992) despite rising sharply during the pandemic. There were 6.7gun murders per 100,000 people (20,958 murders) in 2021, below the 7.2 recorded in 1974. The gun suicide rate, on the other hand, is now on par with its historical peak. There were 7.5gun suicides per 100,000 people (26,328 suicides) in 2021, statistically similar to the 7.7 measured in 1977. The FBI found an increase in active shooter incidents between 2000 and 2021. There were three such incidents in 2000. By 2021, that figure had increased to 61. [16] These statistics alone are evidence that there is something seriously wrong with American society. Then there are some who will say that given the number of people in America, it is normal for some people to have a dysfunctional response to their environment. Is that what you really believe? The truth is that it is not normal. However, the problem is considerably magnified by the fact that mass shootings, suicides, and killings have become a significant part of juvenile and adolescent culture.

Since 2015, over 19,000 people have been shot and wounded or killed in a mass shooting. In 2022 alone, over 600 people were killed, with over 2,700 wounded.
Both the number of mass shooting incidents and the number of people shot in them have increased since 2015, reaching a high of 686 mass shooting incidents in 2021.

There have been more mass gun shootings than there have been days in 2023. As of January 1, to May 1, 2023, more than 13,900 people have been killed in gun violence in the first four months of 2023. More than half of all gun violence deaths this year were deaths by suicide, which is an average of roughly 115 deaths each day. [17]

Fatal Gun Violence in 2023

While school shootings have been a problem for a long time. The Columbine High school shooting in 1999 magnified the problem into the national arena as a serious problem needing attention. Since that time, More than 292,000 students have experienced gun violence in the school environment since Columbine. This is only one area of our society needing corrective attention.

Why is the budget for war and destruction unlimited? Actions that destroy society have no spending ceiling. Why are there budget limitations on education, healthcare, and actions that construct society in ways that would make it better and serve the best interests of humanity? This is a perfect example of backward thinking. This is an example of a weakness in world societies and a misplaced system of values, an indication that the wrong ideologies are governing our world.

Consider the hypothesis that the American society's environmental construct focuses more on individualism, resulting in a modulating behavior pattern where people just don't care about people. People only care about themselves is one hypothesis. Human relationships have deteriorated to the point that people fear people is another hypothesis.

How much do our nation's politicians care about the people in the United States of America? Many politicians want to reduce or eliminate the much-needed entitlement programs, including social security, Medicare, housing assistance, and food assistance. Why should the average American citizen have to work 3-5 years before they vest in a retirement program and receive social security based on their contribution, while elected congressmen have to work only 2 years, or one term in congress, to vest in a pension program, and a senator has to work only 6 years. Each government entity only needs to serve one term before it receives benefits. The law should equally apply. Even our government officials care more about their interests than they do about the interests of the people they serve. The laws they create are unfair in their behalf. Even the politicians who demonstrate concern for the American people support the unfairness of laws and policies passed for their own benefit (that reflect benefits not available to the American people). Any cuts in government spending should first start with entitlement programs and benefits given to Congress and paid for by taxpayers.

Another reason for this book is to reinforce the conceptual reality that even if a person's life is on the wrong path, they can redirect their life circumstances and lived experiences to discover and travel a positive life path. The door to being a decent citizen who contributes positively to society does not close unless the individual chooses to close it. That very same individual can open the door to a positive life whenever they decide. This is evident in the fateful tragedy of Stanley "Tookie" Williams, founder and leader of the Cripts Street gang, who was convicted of murder, sentenced to death, and executed on December 13, 2005. While on death row, he had a catharsis and dedicated the remainder of his life to giving a positive influence to young people. In the final analysis, individuals are agents of their "becoming" and agents to whom they become. However, there is a point of no return. An individual can become so deeply involved in dysfunctional behavior that society offers no forgiveness or repentance in this life. Stanley "Tookie" Williams experienced this fate.

The improvement of American society begins with the improvement of our Kids, students, and young people. Students need to have a clear understanding of the linkage between learning and life experiences; the connection between life experiences and a quality functional life; and the connection between learning, living, and ethical, moral behavior. It seems that many kids, too many kids, are not learning what they need to become contributing members of society.

What issues does that raise for the future prognosis of American society? Therefore, a significant purpose of this book is to give Americans insight into what they themselves can do to overcome the deficiencies in American leadership, the deficiencies in the application of the dogma supporting the rights of all Americans to life, liberty, and the pursuit of happiness. Reacting to the negative characteristics of American society in a negative manner will only take you deeper into the rabbit hole of rights denial and a dysfunctional life. American citizens need to respond to negative America with a positive human Mimesis construction in their lives. This book addresses that issue.

Understanding the concept that the individual can construct their own Mimesis with aforethought and to pass this concept along to future generations will accomplish the intended goal of these four book Volumes.

Definition of Terms used in Volumes I-IV

Aforethought / Forethought - Aforethought" means "premeditated" or "thought of previously". It is most commonly used in the legal context of "malice aforethought," which refers to the intent to commit a crime, particularly murder, that was planned in advance. The phrase distinguishes a planned, deliberate act from one that is impulsive or accidental. i.e. **Forethought.**

Forethought is the act of careful planning or thinking in advance about future actions, needs, or consequences. It involves anticipation, preparation, and prudent consideration to avoid problems and achieve better outcomes. The term can also refer to a specific company.

Attachment Trauma – caused by events and experiences that has a severely emotionally distressing impact on an individual's life and falls outside of the natural human resiliency and natural abilities to cope. When trauma is based on attachment, this suggests a rupture in the parent/child bonding process during the formative years that is not repaired but is perpetuated from one attachment wound to another.

Catharsis - the act or process of relieving a strong emotion (as pity or fear) especially by expressing it in art form. The tragic heroes in Shakespeare plays often experiences a "Catharsis of Emotion" when the tragedy in their life is revealed.

Consciousness - The state of being awake and aware of one's surroundings. The awareness or perception of something by a person. The fact of awareness by the mind of itself and the world.

"Consciousness emerges from the operations of the brain". For general purpose, Consciousness occurs at the time of birth.

Emplotment(s) - the assembly of a series of historical events (Lived Experiences) into a narrative with a plot. In the case of an individual, emplotment(s) are basis for understanding an individual, and for making judgement about their character and personality

Final Mimesis – Death. A time when others continue to reflect on the life of the deceased. How and what do others think about the life lead by the deceased? The cycle of emplotments in an individual's life has ended but their Mimesis will last as long as the memory and thoughts of them prevail.

Future-Orientation Cognition Bias - A future-orientation cognition bias is a human tendency to devote more thought to the future than to the past, especially during spontaneous thought or "mind-wandering". This bias is not always present, however, and can vary depending on the specific cognitive task and across different ages. See Aforethought / Forethought.

Hermeneutics - the study of interpretation, particularly the interpretation of language, whether written or spoken. It's a branch of knowledge that's often used to interpret literary texts, such as the Bible or philosophical works. Hermeneutics is also used in disciplines that deal with the meaning of human intentions, beliefs, and actions, or the meaning of human experience in the arts, literature, and other artifacts.

Hermeneutical Phenomenology - a research methodology and philosophical hermeneutics that combines theory, reflection, and practice to understand lived experiences. It's based on the idea that people are unique because of their life stories, and it focuses on how experiences, traditions, and culture shape people's lives. Hermeneutical phenomenology combines vivid descriptions of lived experience (phenomenology) with reflective interpretations of their meanings (hermeneutics). To give an accurate description of the lived experiences and individual encounters. The same experience may be described differently by different individuals. Each individual has different life experiences and interprets the same phenomena different. Different descriptions of each individuals experience may be different but still accurate and true to that individual. Description of lived experiences accurately is hermeneutical.

Mimesis

(1) In Art and literature Mimesis is the representation or imitation of the real world in art and literature.

(2) Mimesis is also considered another term for mimicry. For example when a human pretends to be an inanimate object in a play for the sake of mimicry.

(3) In literature the three stages of Mimesis recounts the alignment between time and narrative. The two concepts combine to recount the life of an individual in narrative over a finite period time. An individual's life described in narrative over time, according to Riceour, is a means to tell a story about an individual's life. A narrative can also describe how others perceive the life of an individual. The narrative representing an individual's actions and experiences revealed in the three stages of interpretation prefiguration (Mimesis 1), configuration (Mimesis 2) and re-figuration (Mimesis 3)

(4) Mimesis used in terms of the human experience is the perception of the human reality. How an individual perceives themselves, how others perceive the individual and how these perceptions align to form the individuals Mimesis is their Reality. In terms of human, the individuals Mimesis answers the questions: Who are you? Who am I?

Moral Dilemma – When an individual confronts a situation where they want something but are not comfortable with what they have to do to get it? Their dilemma is; the confrontation with making a decision about what to do to get what you want verses what you have to do to get it.

Narrative - an account of related events, such as a story presented through writing, speech, images, or other media. It typically includes a plot, setting, characters, and conflict, and serves to entertain, educate, or convey meaning. Narratives can be factual (like a biography) or fictional (like a novel), and are fundamental to how humans make sense of the world.

Ontology – A concept in metaphysics dealing with the nature of being. The study of how we determine if things exist or not, as well as the classification of existence. It attempts to take things that are abstract and establish that they are, in fact, real.

Phenomenology - the study of phenomena as they manifest in human experience, the way humans perceive and understand phenomena they experience, and of the meaning phenomena have in our subjective experience. Phenomenology is the study of an individual's lived experience they encounter the world during their lifetime.

Phenomena - a rare or significant fact or event. Phenomena is the plural of phenomenon: an exceptional, unusual, or abnormal person, thing, or occurrence. Phenomena represent a number of a series of phenomenon either occurring in relation to one another or as separate unrelated occurrences in the life experiences of human beings.

Phenomenon - a fact or situation that is observed to exist or happen, especially one whose cause or explanation is in question. Something (such as an interesting fact, situation, experience or event) that can be observed and studied and that typically is unusual or difficult to understand or explain fully.

Psychological Theories of Development - Volume 1, Chapter 2, p. 50

Psychosexual Theory of Human Development – Sigmund Freud

Sigmund Freud's theory of psychosexual development proposes that personality is shaped by a person's sexual drives during five stages: oral, anal, phallic, latency, and genital. Each stage is defined by an erogenous zone that is the focus of the libido at that time, and a conflict must be resolved before moving on to the next stage. Unresolved conflicts can lead to "fixation," which can cause certain personality traits and behaviors to persist into adulthood.

Cognitive Development Theory - Jean Piaget

Cognitive development theory, most famously described by Jean Piaget, is the framework for understanding how children acquire and refine knowledge, thinking skills, and problem-solving abilities through a series of four distinct stages. The stages are: sensorimotor (birth to 2 years), preoperational (2 to 7 years), concrete operational (7 to 11 years), and formal operational (12 years and up). According to the theory, children are active learners who construct their understanding of the world through direct interaction and experience.

Social Learning Theory / Social Cognitive Theory - Albert Bandura

Social learning theory, developed by Albert Bandura, proposes that people learn by observing and imitating others, rather than solely through direct experience. This process involves cognitive factors and is influenced by the environment and behavior itself. Key principles include observational learning, modeling, vicarious reinforcement, and the mental processes of attention, retention, reproduction, and motivation.

Attachment Theory - John Bowlby and Mary Ainsworth, psychologist

Attachment theory explains that a strong, early bond with a primary caregiver is essential for development, providing a sense of security that enables exploration and healthy relationships. Developed by figures like John Bowlby and Mary Ainsworth, the theory identifies four attachment styles: secure, anxious (or preoccupied), avoidant (or dismissive), and disorganized (or fearful-avoidant). These styles are shaped by the consistency of the caregiver's responsiveness and impact adult relationships.

Psychosocial Developmental Theory - Erik Erikson

Psychosocial developmental theory, proposed by Erik Erikson, outlines eight stages of human development from infancy to old age, where each stage presents a unique psychosocial crisis. Successfully resolving the conflict between individual psychological needs and social demands at each stage leads to a healthy personality and the acquisition of virtues, while failure can result in difficulties later in life.

Sociocultural Theory - Lev Vygotsky

Sociocultural theory is a framework that emphasizes how social interaction and culture influence cognitive development. Proposed by Lev Vygotsky, it posits that learning is a social process where children internalize knowledge from more skilled individuals, such as teachers, parents, or peers, through social and collaborative activities. Language is a key "psychological tool" in this process, enabling the development of thought as it is internalized from external speech to internal speech.

Reality is a perspective or things in life that are commonly observed and verified to exist, things that are consistent and not random or influenced by conformity or mass hysteria. Something that is perceived as real and is physically experienced by the senses.

Schema is a mental structure to help us understand how things work. It has to do with how we organize knowledge. As we take in new information, we connect it to other things we know, believe, or have experienced. And those connections form a sort of structure in the brain. An individual's **schema** gives a definition / description of who they are. Schema is manifested in behavior.

Social Media - internet-based platforms that allow users to create and share content, build online communities, and interact with one another through text, photos, and videos. It serves various purposes, from personal communication and entertainment to professional networking and political campaigns. Examples include Facebook, Instagram, TikTok, and YouTube, and it has become an integral part of daily life for billions globally, with both positive and negative effects.

Social Referencing - a psychological process that involves using another person's emotional response to an ambiguous situation to guide one's own behavior. Social referencing typically develops between 7 and 10 months of age.

Three-Fold Mimesis of Life – an individual's reality in experiences the three stages in their life.

Stage 1) Coming into being, birth to engagement with others kids in a formal learning environment. The significance of stage 1 is that parents of guardians are the primary and maybe only caretakers. A child's foundational learning takes place in Stage 1.

Stage 2 is the stage where individuals encounter and accumulate lived experiences that further shape and/or reshape their Mimesis.

Stage 3 - is the reflection stage of Mimesis. The individual looks back on their life and evaluates. Others evaluate as well. Stage 3 includes the final Mimesis, death.

Zone of Mimesis Development (ZMD) - takes place over an individual's lifetime from birth during the process of Social Referencing and throughout their lifetime into their Stage 3 Mimesis. ZMD postulates that learning, development and growth is a lifelong process. An individual never gets too old to learn nor does an individual possess complete knowledge. What an individual does have is the ability to construct their Mimesis as agents who make decisions on the phenomena they confront in life.

Zone of Proximal Development (ZPD) - a concept in educational psychology that describes the gap between what a learner can do (learn) on their own and what they can do (learn) with help from another person, a teacher or more capable peers.

Understanding the concept that the individual can construct their own Mimesis with aforethought and to pass this concept along to future generations will accomplish the intended goal of these four book Volumes.

How to read Volume I-IV of the Three-fold Mimesis of Life

The complete works of The Three-Fold Mimesis of Life are over 850 total pages, including all 4 volumes, I-IV, and the Appendix. The readable text in the book is 4 volumes of approximately 650 pages. The author recognizes this is a healthy read for anyone. Volume 1 of the Three-Fold Mimesis of Life is important background information that lays the foundation for understanding the meaning, concept, and evolution of Mimesis, as it is used in all Volumes.

Volume I also addresses the psychological foundation that describes the developmental theories' linkage to a positive Mimesis. Volume 1 is the foundation for understanding the Mimesis construct and profiles of individuals in Volume 3. The Volume 1 background on Mimesis allows the reader to gain insights into how the Theories of developmental Psychology influence Mimesis construction. Volume 1 describes the evolution and concept of Mimesis from Plato to Aristotle to Paul Ricoeur to Dr. Ronald Barnes' (the author) application of Mimeses to the current and future lived experiences and phenomena individuals encounter. Volume 1 gives understanding to the Mimesis of Life as it relates to an individual's lived experiences and insight into the Theories of Psychology that establish the foundation for Mimesis construction. Also included in this Volume is an insight into how the environment acts as a determining factor in Mimesis Construction (lived Experiences and choices), a brief insight into how to break the cycle of dysfunction, and the importance of childhood validation to the development of well-being while constructing one's Mimesis. A healthy positive Mimesis construction provides a stable foundation for a functional life.

Volume 2 discusses the stages of Mimesis in the development process of an individual. The Mimesis of life begins at birth. One might even be able to argue that the Mimesis of Life begins when the fetus is in the womb because research studies indicate that as the developing embryo becomes a fetus, it is impacted by the mother's response to her lived experiences. The fetus develops instincts during gestation. [18] Generally speaking, however, Stage 1 Mimesis begins when a child comes into the world with consciousness but without control or authority over the station or social location in which they are born. There are many aspects of "being born" that are not within the newborn's control, the cultural socialization, the financial status, the place to live, nourishment, and guidance. A baby is born totally dependent on their parents or guardians for survival. Parents or guardians are the initial influence that gives guidance and establishes the initial perspectives the child will embrace. Mimesis, being the representation of an individual's reality, is constantly evolving, developing, and growing as the individual's experiences life, evolves, and grows.

Volume 3 reviews and profiles the lived experiences and Mimesis of noteworthy real-life individuals for the purpose of giving the reader a clear understanding of the concept of Mimesis as it applies to Life. Reader understanding is accomplished by presenting the lived experiences of noteworthy individuals the reader may have familiarity (Volume 3) and relating the lived experiences of these individuals to the concept of Mimesis described in Volume 1. Insight into the Mimesis of familiar individuals, their lived experiences, and how they responded to experiences and phenomena they encountered, how others responded to the individual's Mimesis, and how the individual's environment, in which they exist, influenced their Mimesis, will give the reader clarity on Mimesis and how it relates to their personal situation. The reader will also gain insight into how Mimesis constructs represent the reality of the individual.

Chapter 4 integrates the concept of Mimesis into the Lived Experiences of human beings. The process of living life can be compared to the assembly of a jigsaw puzzle to put the pieces together and make the decisions that determine the construct of the human being. There are many pieces to building a life. It is important to make the right decisions to build a positive life.

The Audience

The audience for these books are:

Parents

The purpose is to give them insight and information on the socialization and development process of raising kids, to inform them of the psychological phenomena to be aware of, and to give a macro insight on how to deal with the issues confronted in raising a child. Being a parent is arguably the most important job in society. School does not teach the responsibility of being a parent. Parents learn "on the job." It is fortunate if individuals, themselves, have good parents. That gives them an advantage in that they have a positive example to emulate. However, many adults who experienced dysfunctional childhoods do not have the benefit of positive role models and, for them, raising a child can be a challenge. Trial and error in being a parent leaves the family vulnerable to situations that can set the child on the wrong course in life. Parenting is a 24/7/365-day job, with no breaks or time-outs. One of the most important things a parent can instill in a child is the ability to make good decisions about the phenomena the child will confront in their lived experiences. When a parent instills, teaches, and trains the child to employ the instincts and concepts of "*Aforethought*" and "*Future-Oriented Cognitive Bias*" when making decisions about the situations, phenomena, and lived experiences they confront, the child starts their Stage 2 Mimesis with an advantage. *"Aforethought"* and *"Future-Oriented Cognitive Bias"* are basic decision-making tools that will guide the individual throughout their life.

Adolescents and Young Adults ages 13-25+

Young people, for the most part, live in the present, in the moment. Youth give little thought to their future until they reach a mature stage, adolescence at the earliest. As toddlers, kids will say they want to be a baseball player, a basketball player, a rapper, a doctor, a lawyer, a police officer, a firefighter, or another profession. However, during the accumulation of lived experiences, career interests change. The thing a young person needs to learn and internalize is the value of making decisions in life that lay the foundation to pursue any positive career choice they make. Bad decisions leading to negative and dysfunctional lived experiences, at an early age, can ruin the future of an individual. For example, if a young person is convicted of theft, it may be difficult for them to get a job in a bank. Early life decisions can make the difference between limited career choices and limited opportunities or numerous career choices and unlimited opportunities. Being able to understand and create the potential for future opportunities in life depends on decisions and behaviors in the past and present.

The continuum of positive decisions and life choices gives the individual direction and standing on how to achieve their goals and objectives in life, with a minimum of encumbering obstacles. Taking responsibility for the decisions the individual makes and realizing you have agency over your lived experiences and life contributes to and determines your Mimesis.

Adults and Mature Individuals

This book gives an introspective insight for adults to understand how their lived experiences and decisions contribute to the people, situations they encounter, and to understand the state/status of their life situation. Understanding that an individual does not have to stay where they are. People can change is a concept that allows the individual to evaluate their life situation and make a determination about their satisfaction level. Who am I? What is my reality? How do others perceive me? How do I perceive myself? Does how others perceive me align with how I perceive myself? This book explores these questions, allowing individual to evaluate their life, the lived experiences they encounter, and the decisions they have made and will make that have framed their past and will determine their future.

Educators of all grade levels (Elementary, Secondary, and Higher Education)

"*The Three-Fold Mimesis of Life*" is relevant for educators at all levels. The four volumes of the "*Three-Fold Mimesis of Life*" can be used as an instructional text to teach psychology or as a guide for parenting, to teach students about the development process of life. The subject matter a student learns is meant to give them knowledge to apply as they proceed through life, into a career, and to become a productive member of society. "*The Three-Fold Mimesis of Life*" can be an effective tool that will contribute to the individual's learning process.

Contents of Volumes I – IV of the Three-Fold Mimesis

Volume I of the Three-Fold Mimesis of Life

Volume I explores the background on Mimesis from its origin with Socrates, Plato, and Aristotle using the concept of Mimesis in artistic forms. In ancient times, human expression conveyed nature's presence in plays and philosophy. Mimesis conveyed humans as representations of nature, using human forms to express nature objects. Such as a humans acting as a tree or a flower.

As Mimesis developed Paul Ricoeur introduced Mimesis as a way to understand characters and meaning in literature. Ricoeur primarily used Mimesis in his theological writings to convey the relationship between lifetime and the narrative of life. Both of which are important for an individual's life to have meaning. The Narrative is a description of the life of an individual's life within the timeframe they live. Time is finite and the lived experiences of an individual (narrative) is created within a confined timeframe. Ricoeur developed this concept in relationship to literature, understanding the plots of a story or narrative of a literary character.

Dr. Ronald Barnes, the author of the four Volumes of the "Three-Fold Mimesis of Life" develops Mimesis to apply to the practical lived experiences of human beings. Humans have the capability to construct their own Mimesis using forethought and understanding how thinking and behavior relates to the narrative of their own life. The foundations created in the developmental process by parents and caregivers weigh heavily in the developmental process of the child. Dr. Barnes applies the concept of Mimesis construction from Birth through death.

Dr. Barnes also links the Developmental Theories of Psychology of noteworthy psychologist as Foundation for Mimesis Construction. Sigmund Freud, Jean Piaget, Albert Bandura, John Bowlby, Mary Ainsworth, Erik Erikson and Lev Vygotsky are psychologist whose research concluded in the advancement of theories of child developmental psychology.

Volume II of the Three-Fold Mimesis of Life

Volume II address the concept of Mimesis Construction from the beginning of Life to the End of Life. While an individual might experience dysfunction in their developmental process and in their early life that does not mean they have to stay in a dysfunctional psychology. *"Where you start is not where you have to stay"*. This concept of Mimesis is applicable to the life of adolescents, young adults and even mature adults. Examples in Chapter III profile of individuals who lives changed because of the decisions they made or did not make. Some lives changed for the better, some change for the worse. The social location an individual is born into does have an impact of their Mimesis construction. The decisions individuals make regarding the lived experiences they encounter are determinate factors in their life projection. The Mimesis individuals construct can also determine the lived experiences they encounter. The evolution of the human narratives are traditionally as follows:

- Birth and dependent on parents and caregivers

- Early childhood influences, nursery school or kindergarten

- Elementary School

- High School

- College / University or the Workforce

  (As the individual grows, their lived experiences expand. Encounters with and exposure to new experiences in life are constant).

- The individual's journey through life is constant until they retire, become senior and reflect on their past.

- Then we die

Volume III of the Three-Fold Mimesis of Life

Volume III profiles noteworthy individuals and explores their life and lived experiences to give the reader a practical insight into Mimesis construction. Another objective is to give the reader insight into how to construct their own Mimesis. Volume III also addresses the following:

- Mimesis: The Representation of the Human Reality

- The Reality of Human Mimesis in Lived Experiences.

- The connection between the Three-Fold Mimesis and Societies Dilemmas

Volume III address the concept of Mimesis being a reflection your reality and the evolution of Mimesis. You do not have to stay when you start. By the reader exploring the lives of noteworthy individuals, the lived experiences they encountered, and outcomes there from; the reader will be able to better understand the concept of Mimesis construction.

Volume III explores the profiles and lived experiences of the following individuals. Additionally, Volume III gives insight into the outcomes they encountered in their life as a result of their Mimesis construction and the decisions they made regarding the experiences they encountered. Volume IV also addresses the environmental impact to their Mimesis construction.

Dr. Martin Luther King, Jr., Muhammad Ali, Oprah Winfrey, Barack Hussein Obama, Billy Graham, Queen Elizabeth II, Richard Nixon, Malcolm X, Stanley "Tookie" Williams, Donald Trump, Jay-Z, Tupac Shakur, Elvis Presley, Beyonce, Marilyn Monroe.

Volume IV of the Three-Fold Mimesis of Life

"Your Mimesis is when how you perceive yourself aligns with how others perceives you". Volume IV addresses Mimesis Construct Challenges and Dilemmas. Mimesis Construction is not a haphazard activity. It requires forethought and behavior that aligns with the individual's thinking. Even then, there are environmental influences on Mimesis construction. The economy, politics, education, work opportunities, family, friends, and other experiences and influences the individual will encounter has they live life. How your Mimesis is constructed will determine how you respond to the societal influences, challenges and dilemmas.

Understanding the concept that the individual can construct their own Mimesis with forethought, and to pass this concept along to future generations will accomplish the intended goal of these four book Volumes.

Your Mimesis is Your Reality "When how you perceive yourself, aligns with how others perceive you"

References

[1] *Weissbourd, R., Batanova, M., Torres, E., McIntyre, J., and Eskander, S. (2021).* Do Americans Really Care For Each Other? What Unites Us—And What Divides Us. *Harvard School of Education.* Retrieved from: https://mcc.gse.harvard.edu/reports/do-americans care-about-each-other

[2] APA (2020). Stress in America 2020: a Mental Health Crisis. *American psychological Society.* Retrieved from: https://www.apa.org/news/press/releases/stress/2 020/report-october

[3] CNN. 10 years.180 school shootings. 356 Victims. *CNN.* Retrieved from: https://www.cnn.com/interactive/2019/07/us/ten-years-of-school-shootings-trnd/

[4] CNN. 10 years.180 school shootings. 356 Victims. *CNN.* Retrieved from: https://www.cnn.com/interactive/2019/07/us/ten-years-of-school-shootings-trnd/

[5] Graf, Nikki (2018). A majority of U.S. teens fear a shooting could happen at their school, and most parents share their concern. Pew Research Center, April 18, 2018.Retrieved from: https://www.pewresearch.org/fact-tank/2018/04/18/a-majority-of-u-s-teens-fear-a-shooting-could-happen-at-their-school-and-most-parents-share-their-concern/

[6] Horowitz, Mirah (2000). Kids who kill: a critique of how the American legal system deals with juveniles who commit homicide. : Law and Contemporary Problems (Vol. 63, Issue 3), Publisher: Duke University, School of Law, Gale Academic Onefile. Retrieved from: https://go.gale.com/ps/i.do?id=GALE%7CA704356 87&sid=googleScholar&v=2.1&it=r&linkaccess=abs &issn=00239186&p=AONE&sw=w&userGroupName =anon%7Eab539463 ;

https://go.gale.com/ps/i.do?id=GALE%7CA7043568 7&sid=googleScholar&v=2.1&it=r&linkaccess=abs&i ssn=00239186&p=AONE&sw=w&userGroupName= anon%7E8f5ca029

[7] Reeves, Richard V. and Holmes, Sarah E. (2015). Guns and race: The different worlds of black and white Americans. Brookings Institution. Brookings Institution. Retrieved from: https://www.brookings.edu/blog/social-mobility-memos/2015/12/15/guns-and-race-the-different-worlds-of-black-and-white-americans/

McCoy, Dana Charles, Raver, C. Cybele, and Sharkey, Patrick (2015). Children's Cognitive Performance and Selective Attention Following Recent Community Violence. Journal of Health and Social Behavior 2015, Vol. 56(1) 19–36 © American Sociological Association 2015 DOI: 10.1177/0022146514567576, jhsb.sagepub.com. Retrieved from: https://www.researchgate.net/publication/2720977 42_Children's_Cognitive_Performance_and_Selective _Attention_Following_Recent_Community_Violence

[8] Gramlich, John (2023). What the data says about gun deaths in the U.S. *Pew Research Organization*. Retrieved from:
https://www.pewresearch.org/short-reads/2023/04/26/what-the-data-says-about-gun-deaths-in-the-u-s/

[9] Reeves, Richard V. and Holmes, Sarah E. (2015). Guns and race: The different worlds of black and white Americans. Brookings Institution. Brookings Institution. Retrieved from:
https://www.brookings.edu/blog/social-mobility-memos/2015/12/15/guns-and-race-the-different-worlds-of-black-and-white-americans/

McCoy, Dana Charles, Raver, C. Cybele, and Sharkey, Patrick (2015). Children's Cognitive Performance and Selective Attention Following Recent Community Violence. Journal of Health and Social Behavior 2015, Vol. 56(1) 19–36 © American Sociological Association 2015 DOI: 10.1177/0022146514567576, jhsb.sagepub.com. Retrieved from:
https://www.researchgate.net/publication/2720977 42 Children's Cognitive Performance and Selective Attention Following Recent Community Violence

[10] Smart, Rosanna, Schell, Terry, L. (2021). Mass Shootings in the United States. Rand Corporation. Retrieved from:
https://www.rand.org/research/gun-policy/analysis/essays/mass-shootings.html

[11] Gun Violence Archive (2023). Mass Shootings in the United States 2023. Retrieved from: https://www.gunviolencearchive.org/reports/mass-shooting

[12] Meyer, Josh (2022). Why are mass shooters getting younger and deadlier? Experts have theories. USA Today. Retrieved from: https://www.usatoday.com/story/news/politics/2022/07/07/mass-shooters-younger-deadlier/7813668001/?gnt-cfr=1

[13] Robb Elementary School Shooting in Uvalde Texas. Retrieved from: https://en.wikipedia.org/wiki/Robb_Elementary_School_shooting

[14] Reeves, Richard V. and Holmes, Sarah E. (2015). Guns and race: The different worlds of black and white Americans. Brookings Institute. Brookings Institute. Retrieved from: https://www.brookings.edu/blog/social-mobility-memos/2015/12/15/guns-and-race-the-different-worlds-of-black-and-white-americans/

McCoy, Dana Charles, Raver, C. Cybele , and Sharkey, Patrick (2015). Children's Cognitive Performance and Selective Attention Following Recent Community Violence. Journal of Health and Social Behavior 2015, Vol. 56(1) 19–36 © American Sociological Association 2015 DOI: 10.1177/0022146514567576, jhsb.sagepub.com. Retrieved from: https://www.researchgate.net/publication/272097742_Children's_Cognitive_Performance_and_Selective_Attention_Following_Recent_Community_Violence

[15] Education Week (2022). School Shootings This Year: How Many and Where. Education Week's 2022 School Shooting Tracker. Retrieved from: https://www.edweek.org/leadership/school-shootings-this-year-how-many-and-where/2022/01

[16] Gramlich, John (2023). What the data says about gun deaths in the U.S. *Pew Research Organization.* Retrieved from: https://www.pewresearch.org/short-reads/2023/04/26/what-the-data-says-about-gun-deaths-in-the-u-s/

[17] Alfonseca, Liara (2023). More than 13,900 people killed in gun violence so far in 2023. *ABC News.* Retrieved from: https://abcnews.go.com/US/116-people-died-gun-violence-day-us-year/story?id=97382759

Everytown (2023) Mass Shootings in the United States. Retrieved from: https://everytownresearch.org/mass-shootings-in-america/

GVA (2023). Mass Shootings in 2023. Gun Violence Archive. Retrieved from: https://www.gunviolencearchive.org/reports/mass-shooting

[18] Fitzgerald, E., Hor, K., & Drake, A. J. (2020). Maternal influences on fetal brain development: The role of nutrition, infection and stress, and the potential for intergenerational consequences. *Early*

---

human development, 150, 105190.
https://doi.org/10.1016/j.earlhumdev.2020.105190.
Retrieved from:
https://www.ncbi.nlm.nih.gov/pmc/articles/PMC74
81314/